Little Mitchie

HYPERSONIC JETS

FUTURE TRANSPORTATION

Joanne Mattern

CREATING YOUNG NONFICTION READERS

Little Mitchie books spark curiosity and support early nonfiction reading for students in Grades 2-3. Designed to build vocabulary, support second language learners, and prepare readers for middle-grade content, each book includes helpful tips for parents and educators to build confidence and deepen understanding of the world.

TIPS FOR READING NONFICTION WITH BEGINNING READERS

Talk about Nonfiction

Begin by explaining that nonfiction books give us information that is true. The book will be organized around a specific topic or idea, and we may learn new facts through reading.

Look at the Parts

Most nonfiction books have helpful features. Our *Little Mitchie* titles include color photographs and graphic aids, a table of contents, a glossary, and an index. Share the purpose of these features with your reader.

Color Photos and Graphic Aids

A lot of information can be found by "reading" photos, charts, maps, and other graphic aids found within nonfiction texts. Help your reader learn more about the different ways information can be displayed.

Table of Contents

Located at the front of the book, this list shows the big ideas within the text and the page numbers where they can be found.

Glossary

Located at the back of the book, the glossary defines key words and phrases that are related to the topic. These words and phrases can be found in the text in colored type.

Index

Located at the back of the book, an index is an alphabetical list of topics and the page numbers where they can be found.

With a little help and guidance about reading nonfiction, you can feel good about introducing a young reader to the world of *Little Mitchie* nonfiction books.

Little Mitchie is an imprint of:

Mitchell Lane
PUBLISHERS

2001 SW 31st Avenue
Hallandale, FL 33009
mitchelllanepub.com

First Edition, 2027.

Author: Joanne Mattern
Designer: Bobbie Houser
Editor: Tricia Hoffman

Library of Congress Cataloging-in-Publication Data
Title: Hypersonic Jets / by Joanne Mattern

Description: Hallandale, FL :
Mitchell Lane Publishers, [2027]

Identifiers:
ISBN 979-8-89260-870-1 (library bound)
ISBN 979-8-89260-967-8 (eBook)

Library of Congress Control Number: 2026936199

PHOTO CREDITS
Alamy: Bill Waterson, 11; RGB Ventures, 15; Dreamstime: Altitudevs, 5; Viktoryvisuals, 20; Public Domain: NASA, 17; Shutterstock: andrey_l, cover, 1, 8; Eliyahu Yosef Parypa, 6; Marc Ward, 13; Scharfsinn, 18; Shutterstock AI Generator, 21; Mike Mareen, 22.

TABLE OF CONTENTS

Chapter One

FAST AND LOUD!

Maria looked up as a jet streaked overhead. “Wow!” she said. She had never seen anything so fast.

A huge boom shook the air.
"What was that?" Maria asked.

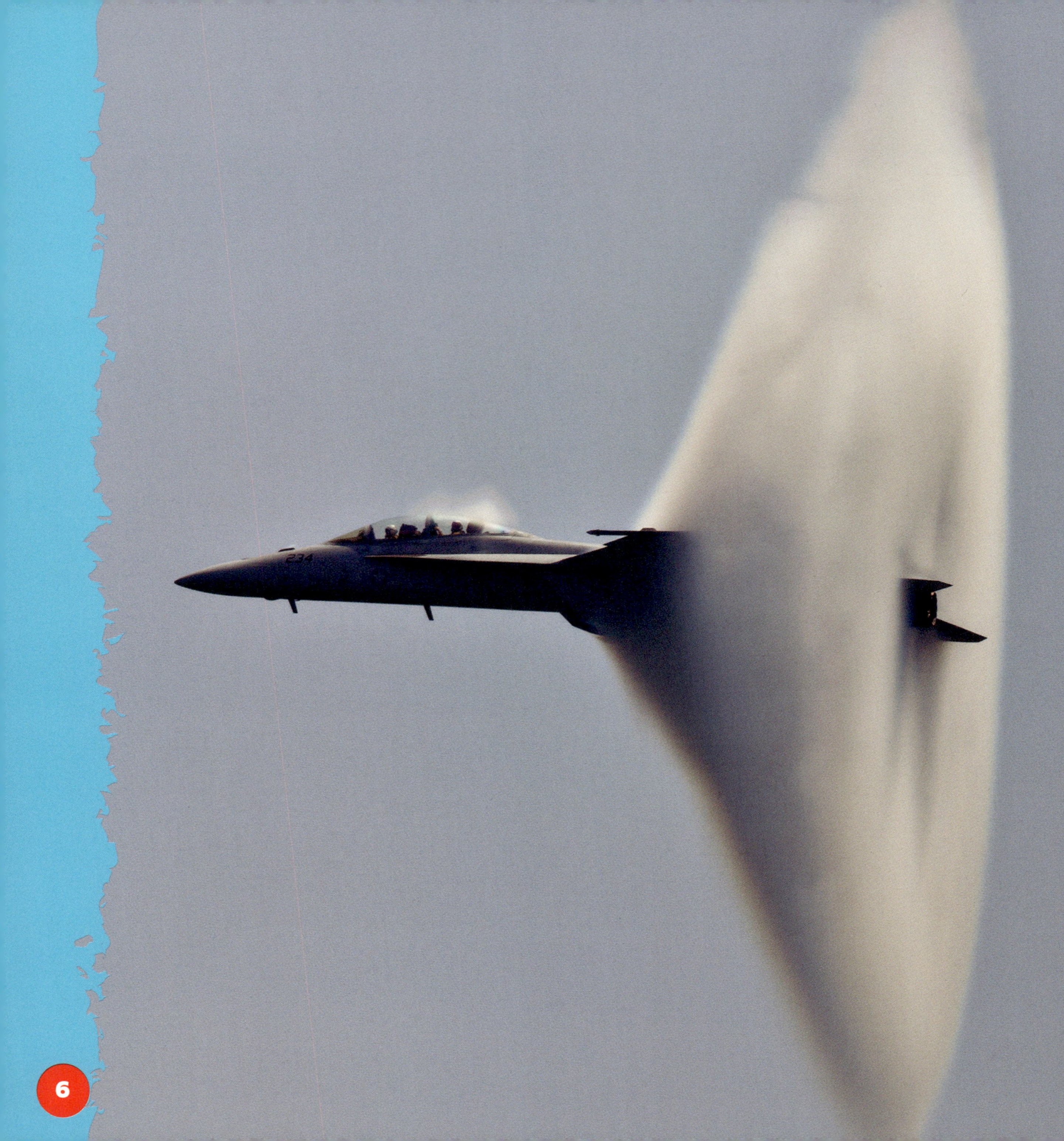

"That was a **sonic boom**," Uncle Carlos explained. "Hypersonic jets fly five times faster than the speed of sound. When they break the sound **barrier**, it makes a booming noise."

"How fast can these jets fly?" Maria asked.

"Hypersonic jets can fly 3,800 miles (6,116 kilometers) per hour," Uncle Carlos said.

SLOWPOKES

Regular jets can fly nearly 600 miles (966 kilometers) per hour. That's fast, but it's a lot slower than a hypersonic jet!

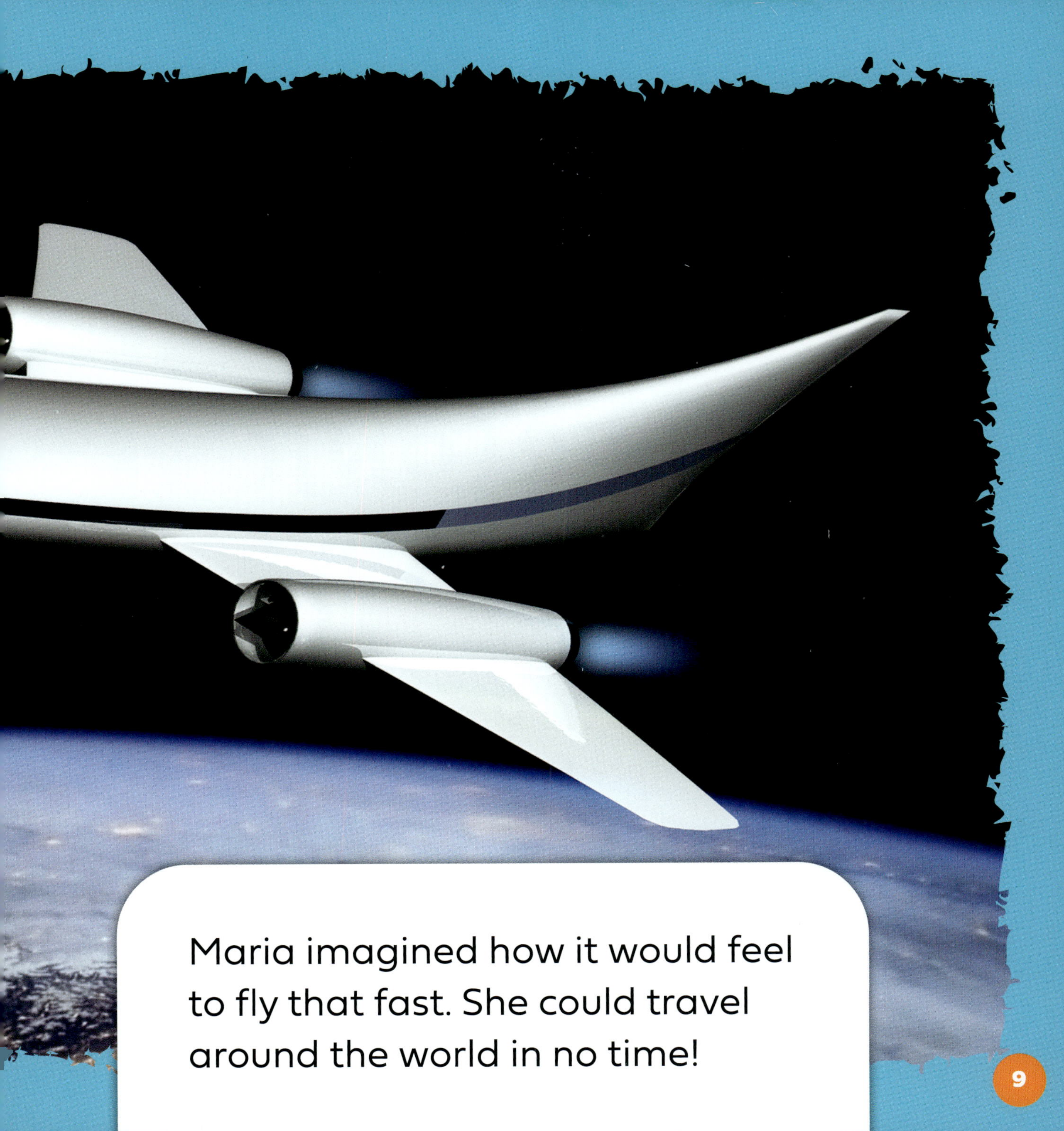

Maria imagined how it would feel to fly that fast. She could travel around the world in no time!

Chapter Two

HYPERSONIC JETS TODAY

Fast planes were an important part of World War II. Afterward, the **military** wanted to fly even faster.

BEFORE THE MOON

Neil Armstrong was the first man to land on the moon. Before that, he flew hypersonic planes.

The first hypersonic rocket plane was built in 1958. It was called the X-15. This plane flew more than 67 miles (108 kilometers) above Earth.

New **technology** helped hypersonic aircraft go even faster. These planes cannot fly on regular engines because they would not work at such high speeds.

HYPERSONIC AROUND THE WORLD

Other countries have worked on hypersonic jets too. Russia, China, and Japan have all come up with new and faster ways to fly.

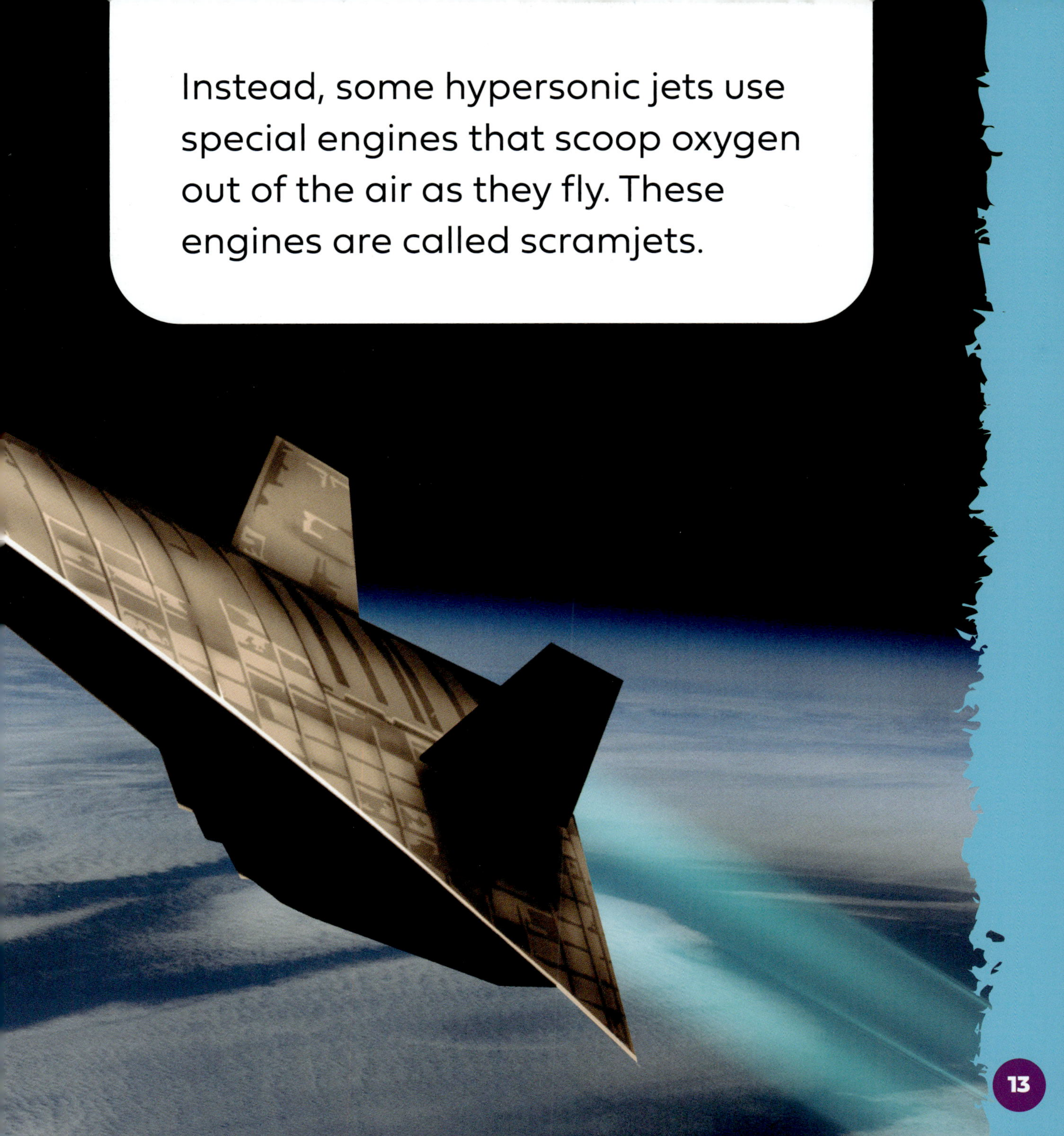

Instead, some hypersonic jets use special engines that scoop oxygen out of the air as they fly. These engines are called scramjets.

The X-43A was a hypersonic aircraft that was designed as a test. It couldn't take off like a regular plane. Instead, a rocket carried it into the air. Once the X-43A reached hypersonic speed, it broke away from the rocket. Then, it could fly on its own for a short time.

SPLASHDOWN!

What happened when it was time for the X-43A to land? It landed in the ocean and broke apart.

Chapter Three

THE FUTURE OF HYPERSONIC JETS

A company called Hypersonix is working on a new type of jet. This jet will be able to fly at Mach 12. That is 12 times the speed of sound!

HYPERSONIX

HYDROGEN

Hypersonix jets can fly fast because they use hydrogen for fuel. Hydrogen burns faster than oxygen and can create more energy.

Hydrogen engines are also cleaner than other engines. They give off **water vapor** instead of gases.

Hypersonic jets aren't ready to carry **passengers** yet. They create a lot of **friction** in the air. Moving so fast can cause parts of the plane to break.

Despite these challenges, people will continue to work on hypersonic jets. The future looks fast!

BIG PRICE TAG

Hypersonic jets are hyper-expensive! It costs about $600 million to build one.

LET'S LOOK AT A HYPERSONIC JET

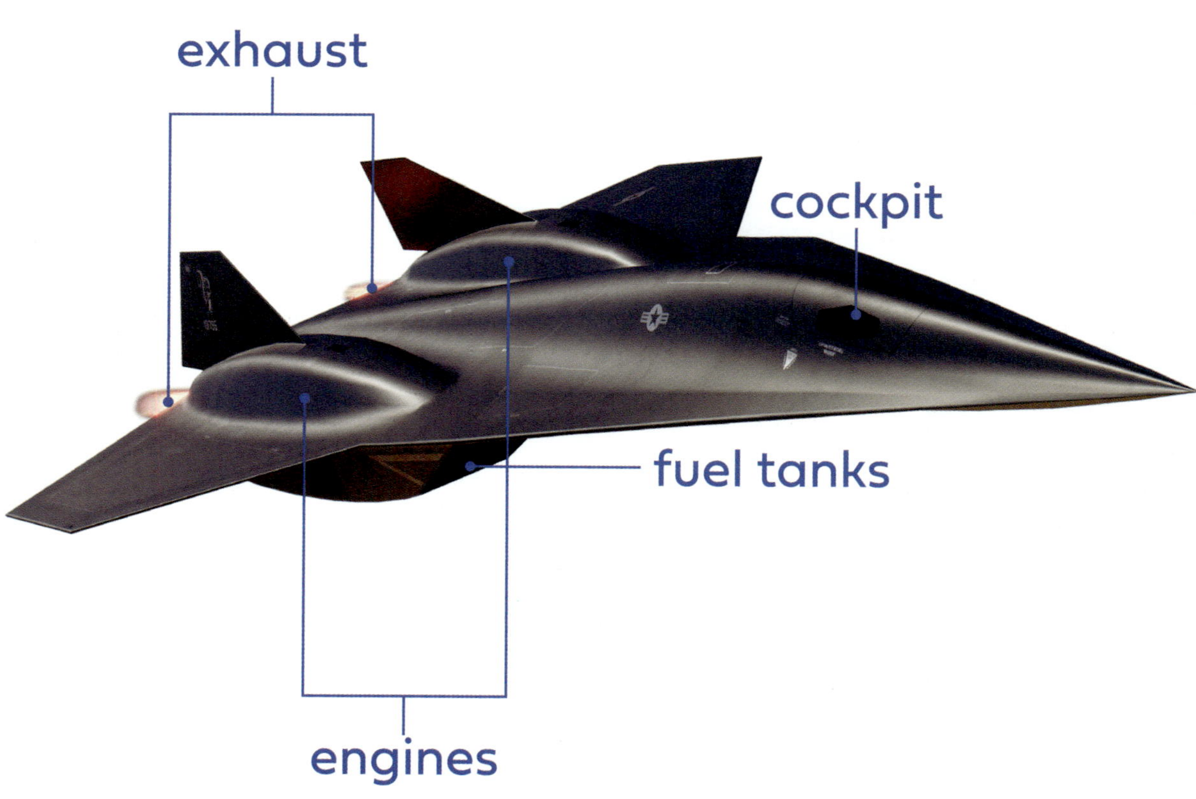

GLOSSARY

barrier (bar-ee-ur) something that blocks other things from going past it

expensive (ik-spen-siv) costing a lot of money

friction (frik-shuhn) the force that slows down objects when they rub together

military (mil-i-ter-ee) a country's armed forces

passengers (pas-uhn-jurz) people who ride in a vehicle

sonic boom (sah-nik boom) a loud sound made when an aircraft flies faster than the speed of sound and breaks through the sound barrier

technology (tek-nah-luh-jee) the use of science and engineering to do practical things

water vapor (waw-tur vay-pur) fine particles of mist or steam that can be seen hanging in the air

FURTHER READING

Henzel, Cynthia Kennedy. *Powerful Military Aircraft.* The Child's World, 2024.

Jensen, Caroline. *Fighter Jets.* Amicus Learning, 2025.

ON THE INTERNET

Hypersonic Facts for Kids
https://kids.kiddle.co/Hypersonic
Learn more about how hypersonic flight works and why these jets create sonic booms.

Jet Aircraft Facts for Kids
https://www.diy.org/article/jet_aircraft
Learn the science behind different kinds of jet aircraft and what makes them fly.

INDEX